CHARLES BRAGG

ON THE LAW

CHARLES BRAGG

ON THE
LAW

Out-of-Court Settlement

A sardonic view
of our fun-filled
legal system
in action

35 images
by Charles Bragg

Introduction by
Pat McCormick

WARNER BOOKS

A Warner Communications Company

Copyright © 1984 by Charles Bragg
All rights reserved.
Warner Books, Inc., 666 Fifth Avenue, New York, NY 10103
Ⓦ A Warner Communications Company

Printed in the United States of America
First printing: November 1984
10 9 8 7 6 5 4 3 2 1

Library of Congress Cataloging in Publication Data

Bragg, Charles.
    Charles Bragg on the law.

    1. Law—Caricatures and cartoons. 2. American
wit and humor, Pictorial. I. Title. II. Title: Bragg
on the law.
NC1429.B733A4   1984   741.5'973   84-7328
ISBN 0-446-38057-1 (pbk.) (U.S.A.)
        0-446-38058-X (pbk.) (Canada)

Hammurabi, in the 18th century B.C. was the sixth Babylonian King of the Amarite tribe. He laid down a remarkable set of laws which became known as the Hammurabian Code.

This code was fantastic for its time and is generally considered the first structured form of law. What is important here is that there is considerable evidence that on King Hammurabi's deathbed he said, "Stop Charles Bragg!" That cry can still be heard today.

Charles Bragg has that laser beam insight that spots the Achilles heel of the pompous and the self-righteous whose balloons need to be pricked.

Although a modest man, Bragg was really steamed when he found out the personalized license plate "GENIUS" was already taken.

What is unique and I sincerely think momentous, is that Charles has combined his gargantuan sense of humor with his fantastic skills as an artist.

Charles Bragg's perspective tells us the "Statue of Justice" can see through her blindfold and has her thumb on the scale.

He is searching for that rarest of creatures—a lawyer with a friend.

If you are in the legal profession and cannot laugh at yourself, do not read on. For the rest of you, you are in for a tasteless romp through that once sacred realm of jurisprudence.

It's wonderful…

Pat McCormick

"The first thing we do, let's ~~kill~~ ^{sue} all the lawyers."

—~~Shakespeare~~
C. Bragg

"I became interested in our legal profession when the government became the chief lawbreaker. Those times [the Vietnam and Watergate years] showed our legal system to be little more than a Circus of Justice. It always seemed a mismatch to me when you oppose the government. In their arsenal are all the laws they have written themselves, and I have discovered how creative and selective they can be when interpreting and enforcing them. (One of my favorites: conspiring to commit a misdemeanor is a felony.) Unfortunately, our legal system has become such a generally inefficient and unwieldy way to work out our human controversies. It's such a perfectly imperfect human thing."

—*Charles Bragg*

"Like those of Bosch and Brueghel, the third B's canvases are crowded with a skyburst of caricatures. Glimpsed through the refracting lens of his imagination, Bragg's world becomes an absurd one, people with gnome-like grotesques and oversized, puffy faces, beady eyes, bulbous noses and broken, jagged teeth.... He dips his brush or pen into the sinful universe and finds much to mock from the lofty to the lowly: politicians, lawyers, doctors, army generals, the hoi polloi. Not even the Pope is spared. And neither is Bragg."

—*Laurie Lucas,* <u>The Press-Enterprise</u>, *California*

The Oath

Cross-Examination

Charles Bragg

Exhibit A

Junior Partner

Process Server

Sanity Hearing

The Indictment

Her Honor

Objection Overruled

Night Court

Recess

Night Court

ACLU

Tort

The Defense Rests

Your Witness

Cross-Examination

"Nolo Contendere"

The Witness

Prosecutor

Closing Argument

Traffic Court

"J'accuse!"

Patent Attorney

Small Claims Court

Court of Appeals

Out-of-Court Settlement

Jury Deliberation

Divorce Lawyer

Objection Sustained

The first art sale I ever witnessed was in 1946. What amazed me, aside from the fact that one could actually sell one's creative work, was that the sale was made by my teenage friend, Charles Bragg.

The transaction took place at the Burnside Billiard Academy, Bronx, New York. No money changed hands. In return for eight humorous drawings of various patrons frequenting the establishment Charles received free pool table time. The drawings were framed and hung right at the entrance. Every day we stopped to admire them as we went to shoot pool.

I relate the above not to tell you of our misspent youth, but to illustrate that Charles Bragg always had an eye for seeing the ridiculous in anything from the local poolroom, our high school, law, religion, the military, to sex, and life in general.

He has been making me laugh for forty years. I read someplace that laughter adds years to one's life. If that's true Charles has lengthened my life considerably. Now it's your turn. If you haven't chuckled or laughed out loud at some of these etchings…you have absolutely no sense of humor. Not to worry. I'm sure Charlie is working on an etching covering that very situation.

He'll get around to you sooner or later.

Gene Light
Editor

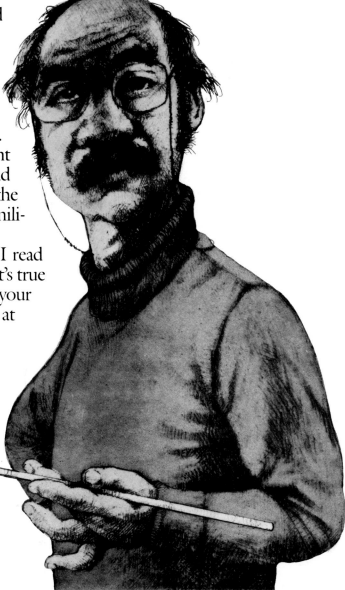